HAPPY EVER CRAFTER
FAIRY TALES

ANNALEES LIM

WAYLAND
www.waylandbooks.co.uk

First published in Great Britain in 2018 by Wayland
Copyright © Hodder and Stoughton 2018

All rights reserved.

Senior Commissioning Editor: Melanie Palmer
Design: Square and Circus
Illustrations: Supriya Sahai

Additional illustrations: Freepik

HB ISBN 978 1 5263 0751 4
PB ISBN 978 1 5263 0752 1

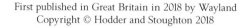

MIX
Paper from
responsible sources
FSC
www.fsc.org
FSC® C104740

Printed in China

Wayland
An imprint of
Hachette Children's Group
Part of Hodder and Stoughton
Carmelite House
50 Victoria Embankment
London EC4Y 0DZ

An Hachette UK Company
www.hachette.co.uk

SAFETY INFORMATION:
Please ask an adult for help with any activities
that could be tricky, involve cooking or handling
glass. Ask adult permission when appropriate.

Due care has been taken to ensure the activities
are safe and the publishers regret they cannot
accept liability for any loss or injuries sustained.

CONTENTS

ONCE UPON A TIME ... 4

COSTUMES AND CHARACTERS 6

ENCHANTED ACCESSORIES 10

PARTY PLANNING 12

INVITATIONS 13

PARTY GAMES 14

PARTY FOOD 16

PARTY DECORATIONS 18

CRAFTY MAKES 22

FAIRY PUZZLE 32

Once Upon A Time ...

Fairy tales are short stories with happy-ever-after endings, making them a perfect bedtime read! Follow the adventures of courageous knights and brave princesses as they travel through enchanted kingdoms, meeting mythical creatures along the way.

It's easy to make these stories come to life in your imagination and you can turn them into a reality, too, by following our simple step-by-step instructions. In this book, you will find out how to transform everyday household objects into magical makes, perfect for decorating your themed parties, as gorgeous gifts for friends and family or just to enjoy all for yourself!

With a sprinkle of fairy dust and just a bit of glue you can make all your crafty dreams come to life. You won't have to 'make believe' when you can make it yourself! Always ask an adult to help you before you start, especially if you are using sharp things like scissors. Remember to cover all surfaces to stop them getting messy with paint or glue, and don't forget to wash your hands when you're finished, too.

FACT!

The Grimm Brothers originally collected stories and folklore from all around Germany. They were the first to start writing them down and sold the first copies of Grimm's Fairy Tales in 1812. The stories have changed over the years to be those we recognise today, and they are still enjoyed by children all over the world.

TOP TIP

Collect things from around the house for your craft supplies. Old magazines and newspapers make great scrap paper, and don't throw away cardboard tubes, plastic containers, jam jars or old food wrappers – they all can be turned into the fantastic fairy tale crafts you will find in this book.

COSTUMES and CHARACTERS

Dressing up is a great way to get into character and turn into the heroes and villains of your favourite books. There are hundreds of different people and mysterious things you can transform into, but if you are stuck, try out these creative costume ideas for size!

MERMAID TAIL

If you can't be under the sea, then this shimmery tail is the perfect way to let you swim around with your friends without getting your feet wet.

YOU WILL NEED:

- A PAIR OF OLD TROUSERS
- FABRIC GLUE • SCISSORS
- CARDBOARD • SHINY FABRIC
- PENCIL • PAINTBRUSH
- (OPTIONAL: WHITECRAFT GLUE AND GLITTER)

1. Lie your trousers out flat and cut off the inside seams.

2. Join the trousers back together again by overlapping the edges and gluing them together.

3. Cut out some U-shaped scales from your shiny fabric and stick on to the trousers using fabric glue.

TOP TIP

If you don't have any spare shiny fabric, make your own. Cover old fabric scraps with watered-down paint. Once dry, paint another layer with a mixture of PVA glue, water and glitter.

4. Draw a tail shape on to the cardboard, then cut out. Decorate the tail shape with more fabric before sticking on to the bottom of the trousers.

FIERY, FIERCE DRAGON

These reptile-like creatures have lots of scales, two flappy wings on their back and a long, spiky tail. But be careful – they also breathe fire!

YOU WILL NEED:

- 2 OLD PILLOWCASES
- SCISSORS • PAINT
- PAINTBRUSH • NEWSPAPER
- SCRAP FABRIC • FABRIC GLUE

1. Use scissors to cut out neck and arm holes from one pillowcase.

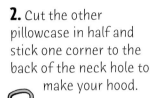

2. Cut the other pillowcase in half and stick one corner to the back of the neck hole to make your hood.

3. Use the leftover pillow material to make your tail. Stick this on to the bottom of the body.

4. Place some newspaper inside the pillowcase before you paint on the scales, eyes, nose and wings.

TOP TIP

If you have more spare fabric, cut up extra triangles and stick them on the back to make a spine of spikes.

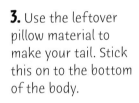

GRRR ...

5. Cut some scrap fabric into triangles. Use pale coloured scraps for teeth, and use two larger pieces for the ears.

7

WIZARD'S CAPE

No wizard is complete without their trusty cape to swish while casting spells. You can decorate yours with shapes and symbols or make up a special crest, so that your wizarding pals can recognise you from afar.

YOU WILL NEED:

- LARGE OLD SHIRT • RIBBON
- FABRIC GLUE • SCISSORS • PAINT
- FLAT PAINT TRAY • OLD JAM JAR (MUST HAVE STRAIGHT, SMOOTH SIDES) • FOAM OR KITCHEN SPONGE
- MASKING TAPE • BUCKET

1. Cut the sleeves from the shirt and glue the seams together to close each hole. Use ribbon or strips from the sleeves to make the cape fastenings. Glue them to the collar and leave to dry.

3. Cut out different shapes using foam or a kitchen sponge. Glue these on to the jam jar.

2. Add some water to paint in a bucket. Try not to make the paint too runny. Soak the shirt until it has all been dyed. Squeeze out the excess paint and hang to dry.

4. Spread paint on to the tray. Roll the jar stamp in the paint so that it is evenly spread on to the foam.

TOP TIP

You can hold the sponge pieces down with masking tape until the glue dries so that the shapes dry flat. Remove masking tape when dry.

5. Roll the jar stamp on to the shirt, printing a continuous design. Leave to dry.

HAIRY, SCARY TROLL

In the Norwegian fairy tale 'The Three Billy Goats Gruff' a scary troll lives under the bridge and gobbles up anyone who tries to cross. Will anyone manage to sneak past you without being caught?

YOU WILL NEED:

- AN OLD WOOLLY HAT • SCRAP FABRIC • FABRIC GLUE • SCISSORS • PAPER • BLACK PEN

2. Cut out a large circle from the scrap fabric and cut in half. Fold over and glue each piece to make a cone.

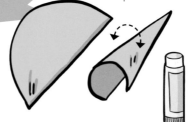

1. Make two eyes from the paper and draw big black pupils on them.

3. Leave to dry before stuffing with other pieces of scrap fabric.

4. Glue the eyes to the front and the cone horns on to the top of the woolly hat.

5. Decorate with long strips of fabric, using the fabric glue to stick them in place.

ENCHANTED ACCESSORIES

If you just need something small to add that finishing touch to your costume, then look no further. Remember you can choose your own colours so that your creations perfectly match your costume.

MAGIC WAND

Every fairy, witch and warlock needs a wand to cast magic spells – you can even make it sparkle in the sunlight.

YOU WILL NEED:

- BOWL • WHITE CRAFT GLUE
- PLASTIC BAGS • TIN FOIL
- GLITTER • COOKIE CUTTER
- WOODEN SKEWER • STICKY TAPE • PUNCHED PLASTIC WALLET • (OPTIONAL: THIN CARD)

1. Pour some craft glue into a bowl and add sparkly things into the mix. Cut up colourful bits of plastic bags, tear up tin foil scraps or pour in some glitter.

TOP TIP

If you do not have a wooden skewer, you can just roll up some card into a thin tube and tape it together instead.

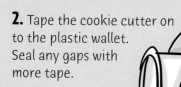

2. Tape the cookie cutter on to the plastic wallet. Seal any gaps with more tape.

3. Pour the glue mixture into the mould. Leave to dry in a warm place. You will know it is dry when all the glue has turned see-through. This could take a few days.

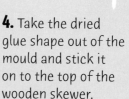

4. Take the dried glue shape out of the mould and stick it on to the top of the wooden skewer.

PARTY CROWNS

Crowns are traditional headwear to show everyone who is in charge of the country. Make these sparkly crowns and you'll be the king or queen of your castle!

YOU WILL NEED:

- CARDBOARD • SCISSORS • STICKY TAPE
- BALLOON • TISSUE PAPER • WHITE CRAFT GLUE • (OPTIONAL: NEWSPAPER, MAGAZINES, PAINT)

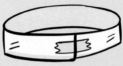

1. Make a cardboard band that fits around your head and another one that is smaller.

2. Blow up the balloon to the size of the larger cardboard band. Tape the balloon inside the band. Tape the smaller band on to the bottom of the balloon to make it stand up.

3. Tear up strips of tissue paper and stick them to the balloon to make the crown. Leave to dry in a warm place.

4. Pop the balloon to remove the crown. Gently bend the crown peaks so they stand up straight. Decorate the crown.

TOP TIP

If you do not have tissue paper you can always use newspaper and paint it after, or use colourful strips of old magazine paper.

PARTY PLANNING

You have your costumes all made but don't get all dressed up with nowhere to go! Parties are a fun way to get together with your friends and celebrate birthdays or special holidays. You can pick one fairy tale as inspiration or mix them all together into one giant fable. Use these top tips to help make your party the best in all the land.

PARTY TICK LIST

☑ **GAMES** Plan to play some fun games to get everyone in the party mood. See page 14 for some inspiration.

☑ **FOOD** Make delicious snacks and drinks that match your theme. See page 16 for some recipe ideas.

☑ **DECORATIONS** Turn ordinary rooms into enchanted realms using simple craft ideas. See page 18 for decorations or page 22 for other crafts you can make.

☑ **INVITE PEOPLE** Send out some invitations so that people remember to turn up to your party – see opposite for a template of what to say, or use the craft on page 19 as an alternative.

GET ORGANISED
To be the best party planner around you will need to get organised. Grab a notebook (or make the Once Upon A Time memory book on page 27) to write down all the important things to remember.

INVITATIONS

Invitations are more than just a nicely decorated piece of paper.
They contain all the important information your guest needs.

To – Write the name of the guest you are inviting.

Dress Code – What sort of outfits do you want your guests to wear? Fancy dress, formal; you decide.

What – Say what sort of birthday party your guests are invited to.

To:

You are invited to my PARTY!

At:

RSVP:

Time:

RSVP – This means you would like your guests to tell you whether they will be coming or not. This helps you to plan how much food to make, how much space you will need and how many party bags to make.

Time – What time will the party start and when will it finish?

Where – Let your guests know where you will be holding the party.

PARTY GAMES

Get the party started with these enjoyably enchanting, themed games. They are quick and easy to make, but will provide you with hours of fun!

CATCH THE GENIE

The most famous tale featuring a genie is the story of Aladdin. Originally a Middle Eastern folk tale, the story tells of a poor boy who lived in China and comes across an evil sorcerer. The story has many different versions but the genie remains a central character in all of them.

YOU WILL NEED:
- PLASTIC BAGS • SCISSORS
- STICKY TAPE • BALLOON
- PERMANENT MARKER PEN

1. Cut the handles off a plastic bag.

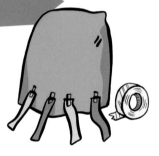

2. Decorate the bag by adding strips of other bags, sticking them on to make some tassles.

3. Draw a face with a permanent marker pen so it looks like a genie.

4. Loosely tape the balloon to the inside of the bag.

HOW TO PLAY

Stand in a circle and choose one person to release the genie. That person blows up the balloon and holds it up high before releasing it. Everyone races to be the first person to catch the genie as it whizzes about. Make the game more of a challenge by getting players to catch the genie with only one hand.

PRINCESS AND THE PEA TOWER

YOU WILL NEED:
- SMALL CEREAL BOX • COLOURED PAPER • SMALL CARDBOARD CUBE (OLD STOCK CUBE BOX) • KITCHEN SPONGES OR FABRIC • SCISSORS • PENS • GREEN TISSUE PAPER

'The Princess and the Pea' was written in 1835 by Hans Christian Anderson. It is a story about a prince who is searching for a real princess to marry. The prince hides a pea underneath a mattress as a test, as only a princess will feel the pea. This game will test you too! Remember that balance is key, as well as keeping your hands steady.

HOW TO PLAY

Players take turns to roll the die. If it shows a number 1 or 2, then you have to stack that many mattresses on to the bed. If it shows a green dot, you have to place a tissue paper pea on the bed. Keep stacking the bed as tall as you can make it. The first to make it topple over loses the game.

1. Cut up small bits of paper and stick them on to the cereal box base to make a collage that looks like a bed frame.

2. Cover all sides of the cube with squares of more coloured paper.

3. Draw a 1, a 2 or a green dot on each side so that you have two sets of each symbol.

4. Roll up lots of balls of green tissue paper.

5. Cut up the kitchen sponges and fabric into different shapes and sizes. You will need lots to play the game, just don't make them too much bigger than the cereal box bed base.

PARTY FOOD

Serve up platters of delicious food at your party and have a real feast. All of these recipes are easy to make and, even better, they do not need to be cooked in an oven.

GINGERBREAD HOUSE

In the story of 'Hansel and Gretel,' two curious children go wandering into an enchanted forest and discover a gingerbread house that belongs to a wicked witch. Make your own version using the chocolate and sweets you love the best – no one will be able to resist your tempting treat.

1. Break one of the chocolate bars in half to make two smaller squares.

3. Using icing pens, decorate the gingerbread men to make Hansel and Gretel or other fairy tale characters. Stick sweets on to the outside of the house and use icing to make doors, windows and roof tiles.

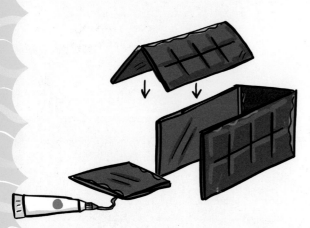

2. Using the icing pens like glue, stick the two squares to the two full bars, to form the base of your house. Glue together the final two bars of chocolate so they form the roof.

SAND-WITCH-ES

Witches were first drawn wearing pointed hats in early fairy tale books in the 1700s, even though they were popular headwear for lots of people in the centuries before. These 'open sandwiches' are so spellbinding that they will be a hit with everyone, too.

YOU WILL NEED:

- BREAD • CREAM CHEESE • HAM
- CHEESE • CHERRY TOMATOES
- SMALL KNIFE

1. Cut the slice of bread in half to make two triangles.

2. Take one triangle and cover it in a thin layer of cream cheese.

3. Cover the tip with a slice of ham. Trim to size if necessary.

4. Cover the bottom in lettuce, making the rim of the hat.

5. Ask an adult to help cut some slices of cheese. Add a slice to the top to make the band and half a cherry tomato for the buckle.

TOP TIP

Change the toppings to what you like and make different designs. You can use sweet or savoury ingredients to make a big selection for your guests to choose from.

PARTY DECORATIONS

These crafts can help you create the perfect party atmosphere for you and your guests to enjoy. Make decorations, invitations and more, all with a fairy tale twist!

How did Jack know how many beans his cow was worth?
He used a cow-culator!

BEANSTALK TABLE DECORATIONS

'Jack and the Beanstalk' is a popular story, especially for Christmas pantomimes. Jack trades his cow for some beans that magically grow into a very tall beanstalk. He climbs up the beanstalk but when he reaches the clouds he discovers a giant's castle in the sky.

YOU WILL NEED:
- PAPER CUPS • NEWSPAPERS
- MASKING TAPE • GLUE • GREEN PAINT
- PAINTBRUSH • GREEN TISSUE PAPER
- SMALL PLASTIC BAGS • RICE/DRIED BEANS

1. Paint the paper cups in bright colours and leave to dry.

2. Twist sheets of newspaper into a beanstalk shape and hold in place with masking tape. Paint the stalks green and leave to dry.

3. Fill some plastic bags with rice or dried beans, and place in the bottom of the cups.

4. Stick the beanstalk on top of the bags of beans/rice. Decorate with tissue paper bean pods, spirals and leaves.

RAPUNZEL'S TOWER INVITATIONS

The story of 'Rapunzel' is hundreds of years old and has been told in many different ways by different authors. A very early version seems to have been based on Saint Barbara who was locked away in a tall tower by her father but, unlike the tales told today, her hair definitely was not long enough to help her escape.

YOU WILL NEED:

- OLD BIRTHDAY CARD • COLOURED PAPER
- WHITE PAPER • SCISSORS • COLOURED PENS
- GLUE STICK

1. Fold the white paper and then cut to size. Cut two bits of coloured paper that are the same size as your card. Cut one piece from white paper that is slightly smaller.

2. Take the white sheet of paper and fold it in half. Cut three lines as shown.

3. Push the cut-out sections inwards and close the card to crease the sections. This will create a pop-up effect when the card is opened.

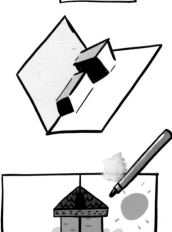

4. Decorate the pop-up sections to make them look like a tower and a roof.

TOP TIP

Add a wool plait that hangs out of the middle of the window to look like Rapunzel's long locks of hair.

You are invited ...

5. Stick each side of the card on to one of the coloured pieces of paper you cut out earlier.

19

GOBLIN GOBLETS

Gulp down delicious homemade punch in style with these precious party cups.

YOU WILL NEED:

- CLEAR PLASTIC WINE GLASSES
- MULTI-COLOURED PERMANENT MARKER PENS • TIN FOIL
- GLUE STICK

1. Rip the tin foil into small pieces. Stick them on to the base and stem of the glass using the glue stick.

2. Draw and colour in shapes on the bowl of the glass.

3. Go over the top of these shapes in a contrasting colour, drawing geometric lines to make the shapes look like gems.

REMEMBER

Do not decorate your goblets to the very top – you need to leave space so you can drink out of them safely.

PERFECT PUNCH RECIPE

With help from an adult, cut up lots of fruit (lemons, oranges and strawberries work well) and put in a large bowl. Add some orange juice, pineapple juice and lemonade until the bowl is full. Squeeze in some fresh limes and mix it all together. Place some ice into your goblets and pour in your punch using a ladle.

FROG PRINCE CAKES

In this tale, an evil witch casts a spell on a prince and turns him into a frog. Only a kiss from a princess can reverse the magic. Could you be the one to break the spell?

YOU WILL NEED:

- 1 SMALL MADEIRA CAKE
- 2 TABLESPOONS OF READYMADE CHOCOLATE BUTTERCREAM
- GREEN HARD-BOILED SWEETS
- PLASTIC BAG • ROLLING PIN
- YELLOW FONDANT ICING
- GREEN CAKE CASES • SCISSORS

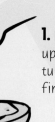

1. Break the sponge up with your fingers, turning it into a fine crumb.

2. Little by little, add some buttercream to the crumbs and mix until it turns into a dough.

3. Place the sweets in a plastic bag and crush them gently into a fine sugar using the rolling pin.

Make some crowns from the fondant icing and press on to the heads of the frogs.

TOP TIP
Flatten out some cake cases, and cut out a 'V' shape out of each of them. Put the cakes on top so it looks like frogs sitting on lily pads.

4. Mould the dough into frog shapes and dip into the crushed sugar mix to give them a shimmery coat.

CRAFTY MAKES

Creating your own toys and decorations is so much fun and you can personalise them too, making each one truly unique. Follow these simple step-by-step instructions to create lots of fairy-tale-inspired crafts, perfect as gifts but even better to keep.

FAIRY GARDEN

These tiny winged creatures are often hard to spot, so why not make your own and clip them to things around the house. Keep an eye on them as you never know what they might get up to when you're not looking!

YOU WILL NEED:

- WOODEN PEGS • PAPER
- FLAT PLASTIC LID • SWEET WRAPPERS • MARKER PEN
- SCISSORS • WHITE CRAFT GLUE

1. Draw and colour in a fairy head and body.

2. Cut it out and turn over to colour in the other side.

3. Draw some wings on to the plastic and carefully cut out.

4. Decorate the wings with torn up pieces of sweet wrappers and glue them on.

5. Glue the fairy body to one flat side of the peg, and the wings to the other side. Leave to dry.

Why can't you give Elsa a balloon? Because she will 'Let it go'.

THREE BEARS

Goldilocks stumbles across a house in the woods but she does not realise that the three bears live there. She eats their porridge, tries their chairs and sleeps in their beds. Once you have made your own bear family, try making the other things in the story so you can act out this famous tale yourself.

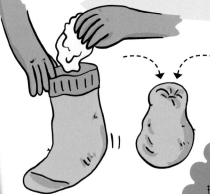

1. Fill the sock with the toy stuffing and stuff the remainder of the sock inside itself so no stuffing escapes.

TOP TIP
Follow the steps twice more, so that you make all three bears but make sure you use socks of different sizes, so that the bears are different sizes, too.

2. Loosely wrap the elastic band around the top to make the head.

3. Tightly wrap more elastic bands to make 4 small balls. These will be the hands and feet.

4. Cut out ears and a face from the felt and stick on to the bear's head.

5. Use the permanent marker to draw details on the face, such as the eyes, nose and mouth.

GIANT'S LEGS

'Fee-fi-fo-fum' is the traditional call from the giant in the story of 'Jack and the Beanstalk.' Surprise your guests by making a giant to greet them when they arrive at your party!

YOU WILL NEED:
- 2 COAT HANGERS • WHITE PLASTIC BAGS
- THIN CARD • STICKY TAPE • BLUE PAINT
- SCISSORS • PERMANENT MARKER

1. Paint lots of sheets of card blue on both sides and leave to dry before folding like a corrugated fan.

2. Stick the sheets of folded card together using tape. Join enough pieces together so they reach the ceiling. Make two strips.

3. Tape these long strips onto a hanger each, to make the giant's legs.

4. Scrunch up some plastic bags and fix them to each hanger to hide them and make them look like clouds.

5. Make some shoes using more of the card, drawing on details with permanent marker. Stick them on to the end of the legs. If time, you could also make a pair of arms, as shown below.

TOP TIP

Make two more hangers to go either side of the legs, for the arms. Hook them all on to a curtain pole to make your giant.

ENCHANTED CASTLE SNOW GLOBE

YOU WILL NEED:
- JAM JAR AND LID • GLITTER • WATER
- FLAT PLASTIC LID • SCISSORS
- PERMANENT MARKER PENS • GLUE
- RED AND GREEN TISSUE PAPER
- MODELLING CLAY

In the story of 'Sleeping Beauty,' as soon as the princess pricked her finger on a spinning wheel she fell into a deep sleep. The whole castle fell under the spell too, falling asleep where they stood, leaving the castle still and overgrowing with plants for many years. Make your own enchanted castle that you can shake. Do you think you can wake up everyone inside?

1. Press some modelling clay on to the inside of the jam jar lid.

2. Cut out a castle shape from a plastic lid and colour in using the permanent marker pens.

3. Press the castle into the plasticine, making sure it is very secure.

4. Fill the jar with water and glitter and carefully screw on the lid.

5. Turn the jar over and cover the joins with green tissue paper and glue to make overgrown vines. Roll up small red balls to make roses.

STORY MEMORY BOOK

All great stories start with 'Once upon a time'... but what happens after that is up to you! Make your own book and fill it with old pictures and notes on what adventures you have been on. What will be your favourite chapter?

YOU WILL NEED:

- SCRAP PAPER • HOLE PUNCH
- STRING • THICK CARD • WRAPPING PAPER • WHITE CRAFT GLUE

1. Pile the papers on top of each other and make some holes using the hole punch. Feed the string through the holes to bind the pages together. Remember to tie the string at both ends so that it does not come loose.

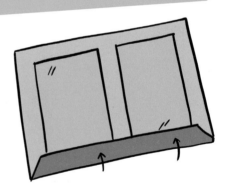

2. Make a cover from thick card that is slightly bigger than the pages of the book. Glue the pages on to the wrapping paper. Fold the cover over and glue the edges.

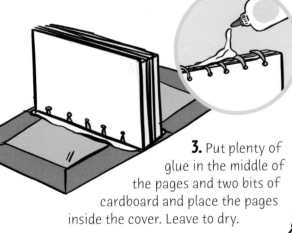

3. Put plenty of glue in the middle of the pages and two bits of cardboard and place the pages inside the cover. Leave to dry.

4. Decorate the cover with cardboard corners and put a sign in the middle to add the title of your story.

FAIRY LIGHTS

You won't need to find fairy dust to make these fairies sparkle in the dark – these magical creatures light up using LED lights. If you don't have any LED lights, you can hang your fairies in the window and watch them catch the sunlight.

YOU WILL NEED:
- PLASTIC BOTTLES AND LIDS • STICKY TAPE • SCISSORS • LED LIGHTS
- SWEET WRAPPERS/SHINY PAPER
- PERMANENT MARKER PEN

1. Cut your bottles in half and cover the edges with sticky tape to make sure there are no sharp bits.

2. Place the bulb on to the neck of the bottle and fix the wire in place using sticky tape. Do not cover the bulb.

3. Decorate the bottle with layers of sweet wrappers or shiny paper, fixing them in place with sticky tape.

4. Draw a face on the bottle lid with the permanent marker pen and add sweet wrappers or shiny paper for hair. Make some wings from the bottom of the cut bottle. Cover the edges with sticky tape and decorate.

5. Ensure all fairy bottles are attached securely to the wire, then hang them up and enjoy the sparkle!

MAGIC MIRROR

The Evil Queen in 'Snow White' has her very own enchanted mirror. It tells her who is the fairest in the land when she looks into it and says the magic spell. What will yours say to you?

Why was Cinderella no good at playing tennis?
Because she was always running away from the ball!

1. Cut out a mirror shape and a wide border using the thick card.

2. Scrunch up shapes made from newspaper and tape them to the mirror base to make the face.

3. Spread a thin layer of glue over the mirror base and shapes. Cover with the tin foil.

4. Gently press down the tin foil so it covers all the shapes and reveals the face.

5. Stick on the border and colour any bare cardboard with paint.

MINI KINGDOMS

Each fairy story is based in a different realm of a magical kingdom. Bring all the stories together by making mini story boxes filled with your favourite characters. They are stackable so you can create a whole wall of make-believe that you have bought to life.

YOU WILL NEED:

- SMALL BOXES (OLD SHOE BOXES ARE PERFECT) • PAPER • CARD • PENS
- SCISSORS • GLUE STICK

TOP TIP

If you are not confident in drawing the characters for your story boxes, then why not look through any magazines you have and cut out characters from there? You can also print some from a computer.

1. Cover the box in one colour. This can be done by cutting the paper to the size of the sides and gluing them in place.

2. Draw the scenery and characters on to the paper and card. When you cut them out, remember to leave tabs on, so that it helps you to stick them in place.

3. Stick them all in place using the glue stick. If you want to make some moveable, stick them on to a thin card base and place into your scene.

What Story?

In one box, you can place the tall beanstalk that reaches the giant's home in the clouds; in another, you can set an underwater scene where a little mermaid can swim about. Create magical forests where you can hide cunning trolls amongst the trees or discover a witch's gingerbread house. And don't forget to make a big castle for all your knights to live in before they ride off visiting faraway lands! If you're stuck for any more ideas, just open your favourite collection of fairy tales and use the stories as inspiration.

FAIRY PUZZLE
CAN YOU FIND THE ANSWERS TO THESE QUESTIONS?

1. How many stars can you find in the picture?

3. Which is the odd unicorn out?

2. Where is the gnome hiding?

4. How many rubies can you spot?

A

B

C

D

ANSWERS: 1. 14 stars **2.** Behind the beanstalk **3.** C **4.** 6 rubies

DISCOVER MORE...

HAPPY EVER CRAFTER

978 1 5263 0753 8

Realm of Knights and Castles
Kingdom of Costumes
King of the Castle
Invitations
Party Games
Party Decorations
Fantastic Feasts
Medieval Makes
Knights Puzzle

978 1 5263 0755 2

Sci-Fi Worlds
Outer Space Outfits
Planet Party
Intergalactic Invites
Party Games
Party Decorations
Space Food
Crafty Makes
Space Puzzle

978 1 5263 0751 4

Once Upon a Time
Costumes and Characters
Enchanted Accessories
Invitations
Party Games
Party Food
Party Decorations
Crafty Makes
Fairy Puzzle

978 1 5263 0713 2

Argh M' Hearties!
Daring Dressing Up
Pirate Plans
Invitations
Party Games
Party Decorations
Party Food
Crafty Makes
Pirate Puzzle

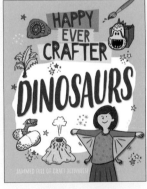

978 1 5263 0757 6

Dinosaur World
Big Beasts Fancy Dress
Prehistoric Party Plans
Invitations
Party Games
Party Decorations
Party Food
Craft-o-saurus
Dinosaur Puzzle

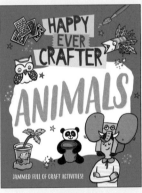

978 1 5263 0759 0

Amazing Animals
Cute Creature Costumes
Party Animal
Invitations
Party Games
In the Zoo
Tasty Treats
Creature Crafts
Animals Puzzle

WAYLAND
www.waylandbooks.co.uk